DETERMINERS IN ENGLISH

SHARPEN YOUR SKILLS ON THE USE OF A, AN, THE AND OTHER DETERMINERS

ADITYA KUMAR PANDA

ISBN 979-888546440-6

For my daughter Nini

Contents

Preface

Preface (1st Edition)

According to the linguists, all the words of a language can be grouped into two categories, one is function, and another one is content. All the function words are closed group words and all the content words are open group words. Articles, determiners, preposition, quantifiers are function words whereas nouns, adjectives, adverbs, verbs are considered as the content words. Out of these two groups, it is the group of function words which occurs more frequently than the content words in a language. Every language has the expression of definiteness and indefiniteness which come under determinatives. In the history of a language, there are words which are used more compared to other words in the same language. In English language, the frequency of use of the articles is more. There was an analysis of the English corpus over 2 billion words which has to determine the frequency of words in English. It is found from this analysis that the first ten most commonly used English words are: the, be, to, of, and, a, in, that, have, I (http://www.oxforddictionaries.com/words/the-oec-facts-about-the-language). These words belong to article, preposition, conjunction, pronouns. Most commonly used top 100 words in English are function words.

Many of the top 100 frequently used words in English are determiners. Determiners fall under the category of function words. The Oxford Concise Companion to the English Language defines a determiner as *a part of speech or word class that determines or limits a noun phrase, showing whether a phrase is definite or indefinite..".* The Oxford

Dictionary of Linguistics defines it *as limiting the potential referent of a noun phrase.*Determiners are used before noun and they are the referents of the nouns. Traditionally, they are known as the limiting adjectives. Etymologically, it refers to mark a boundary on something or limiting something. Martha Kolln and Robert Funk write that "*the Determiners signal nouns in a variety of ways: They may define the relationship of the noun to the speaker or listener (or reader); they may identify the noun as specific or general; they may quantify it specifically or refer to quantity in general*". A determiner is an indicator of quantity, definiteness, indefiniteness, position of a noun in a sentence.

In this book, I have divided the English determiners into six categories: Definite Article: the, Indefinite Articles: a and an, Demonstratives: this, that, these, those, Possessive Pronouns: my, your, his, her, its, our, your, their, Quantifiers: some, any, few, little, more, much, many, each, every, both, all, enough, half, little, whole, less, Other determiners: either, neither, numerals like one, two, twenty, 1, 2, 20, first, second, etc. There is an exercise given at the end of each of the chapters. The first chapter has its exercise on the end of the second chapter.

The book will be useful for the school and college students who want to learn about the usage of the English determiners. The scope of the use of the book does not limit to the students only, anyone who wants to refresh his/her skills in the usage of the English determiners can get benefitted from the book.

Aditya Kumar Panda
Central Institute of Indian Languages
Mysore-570006

Preface to the 2nd Edition

I think that the grammar of a language is the finite set of rules that generates infinite set of sentences. I have got this idea from Noam Chomsky's *Syntactic Structures*. Every native speaker of a language is equipped with the finite set of rules through which he/she can express infinite number of sentences throughout his/her lifetime. One of the major chunks of the finite set of rules is associated with the most frequently used determiners in a language. And English, a major world language, is not an exception here, it has determiners which are most frequently used functional words in British English-American English-Indian English-Australian English so on and so forth. It always strikes my mind to discuss these determiners with students/friends/teachers and I find it interesting to note the usage of these determiners. It is a fact that functional words do not change as much as the content words but language is an open-ended entity that can mount to influence the functional words. This book is a small introduction of the basic rules of the determiners in English. Hope readers will refresh and sharpen their grammar skills.

Aditya Kumar Panda
Mysore, 25th December, 2021

CHAPTER ONE

Definite Article: The and its uses in English

Definite reference is expressed through the function words in a language. Such words are used in many contexts in a particular language and the frequency of their uses is also more. In English, the definite reference is expressed through the use of the definite article, 'the'. It has a number of uses in English. It is used in the following contexts:

A. As it is a definite article, it is used before a definite expression (singular or plural) in a sentence.

The boy is a thief.
The girl in red dress is my sister.
The birds are chirping in the tree.
The students in an English class at my school were asking difficult questions.

B. 'The' is used before a thing already mentioned in communication.

The mouse is running which you saw yesterday.

The cricket match between Australia and India was cancelled.

We met the boy who was playing on the ground.

'The' is used before both singular and plural noun, when the noun is specific.

Did you see the boys who were playing cards ?

The people in the hall are overjoyed.

C. It is used before the unique objects like the Moon, the Sun etc which are known to everyone and only one such object exists.

The Sun gives us light on the earth.

Last night, I was looking at the Moon.

Earth takes 'the' before it when it refers to the land area where we live in but it does not take 'the' before it when it refers to the planet.

D. The is also used before the names of the well-known work of art:

The Taj Mahal
The Konark
The Khajuraho
The India Gate

E. The is used before the official residence of a king, a president and a prime minister:

The White house
The Rashtrapati Bhavan
The Royal Palace of Madrid

F. The is used before the names of famous and classical books:

The Bible
The Bhagvad Gita
The Quran
The Vedas
The Guru Granth Sahib

G. Before superlatives and ordinal numbers:

The biggest building
The best student
The first chapter
The last page
The fifth king
The seventh son

H. When an adjective or odinal numeral is used post-positionally, 'the' is used for emphasis before them: King Richard the Second, Henry the Fourth, Alfred the Great.

I. It is used before the adjectives referring to a whole group of people:

The American
The old
The Chinese

J. 'The' is used when we refer to a noun in a generic sense:

The tiger is a four -legged animal (All tigers are four-legged).

Articles can be used to refer to the whole class to which individual countable nouns belong.

An elephant is a big animal. (Any elephant)

The elephant is a big animal. (all elephants, elephant as a generic category).

K. It is used to refer to a part of the body or personal belonging (in place of possessive pronouns like my, your, his/him/her):

He was injured in the right leg.

She will take me by the hand.

L. Before decades or group of years:

The eighties

The sixties

The seventies

M. We don't use 'the' before (proper) names like Raja, Rahim, Stephen, Pakistan, Brazil

N. We use 'the' when the name includes the words like kingdom, union, states and republic:

The United States of America

The United Kingdom

The Republics of the Soviet Union

The State of Illinois

The Republic of the Congo

The Union of Soviet Socialist Republics

The United Arab Emirates

The Kingdom of Bahrain

O. We use 'the' before the names of the mountain ranges, group of islands, rivers, seas, ocean, forests, deserts :

The Himalayas
The Atlantic Ocean
The Arctic Ocean
The Mahanadi
The Godavari
The Canaries
The Sahara Desert
The Kaveri
The River Thames
The Hindu Kush
The Mississippi River
The Andaman and Nicobar Islands
The Mediterranean Sea
The Red Sea
The Gulf of California
The English Channel
The Kara Sea
The Daintree Rainforest
The Sundarbans
The Antarctic
The Pacific Ocean
The Arabian Sea
The Atlantic Ocean
The Bay of Bengal

P. 'The' is used before the names of the newspapers, journals, periodicals:

The Times of India
The Hindu

The Indian Express
The Times
The Dainik Jagran
The Deccan Chronicle
The Washington Post
The New York Post
The Chicago Tribune

Q. 'The' is used before the names of the organizations:

The University Grants Commission
The English and Foreign Language University
The University of Delhi
The University of Oxford
The United Nations Educational, Scientific and Cultural Organization
The University of Heidelberg
The Massachusetts Institute of Technology
The Indian Institute of Technology
The Indian Council of Social Science Research

Generally, 'the' is used before the names of the organizations that start with the words like university, institute and it is a long one. In case of the names of the organizations that start with the proper name, 'the' is not used: as for examples: Stratford University, Jawaharlal Nehru University, Jadavpur University, New York University, Peking University

R. Definite article is not used with the acronyms that are pronounced like words but it is used before the initialisms that pronounce letter by letter:

UNESCO (the UNESCO is unacceptable), NATO (the NATO is unacceptable)

The USSR (only USSR is unacceptable), The USA (USA is unacceptable)

'The' is not used before university, institute acronym: it would be grammatically wrong if one says, the MIT (unacceptable), the JNU (unacceptable).

S. The is used before the names of the countries who have plural names:

The Philippines
The Maldives
The Netherlands

T. 'The' is used before the adjectives which refer to the groups of people:

The poor will suffer the most. (the poor means the poor people)

The rich get richer. (the rich means rich people)
The Japanese (people from Japan)
The Chinese (people from China)
The old (old people)
The young (refers to the people who are young)
The elderly (elderly people)

U. We use 'the' before the musical instruments:

My niece is learning the guitar.
We were playing the violin.
The flute, the tabla
The drum

The piano
The banjo
The pump organ

V. Before the names of house, restaurant, hotels:

The Vintage Villa
The Izmailovo Hotel

W. Before the names of the families, 'the' is used:

The Birlas
The Obamas
The Stephens
The Washingtons
The Matthews

X. 'The' is used when referred to the whole of transportation system or communication system:

People use the telephone system.
We also use 'the' before the means of transport.
How long does it take on the bus?
The bus to the city is at 10 AM.

When we refer to a transport system indefinitely, we don't use 'the',

They go to the office by bus.
They arrived by car.

Y. We use 'the' before human institutions which we attend, use or observe:

You are going to the church (place of worship).

The lunch (items) is good.

But when we talk about the activity or the primary purpose, we don't use the definite article:

She goes to church on Sundays. (Purpose of praying)

We will have lunch together.

We don't use 'the' before lunch, dinner, breakfast, supper. But when these words do function as the adjectives, 'the' is used before them:

He was sitting nearby the lunch table.

The dinner party would be interesting.

Z. 'The' is used before the names of the currencies: the US dollar, the Yen, the Rupee, the Iraqi Dinar, the Ruble, the Euro

AA. 'The' is used before the names of the days, months which are definite:

Do you remember the Sunday when I met you?

The March of 2016 was very hot.

We don't use the definite article before the names of days, months which are general or indefinite:

He will come on Monday.

The film will be released in August.

BB. 'The' is also used differently in different varieties of English: while referring to a sports team, the British omit the definite article, 'the' but, the Americans use it:

Manchester United (British)

The New York Yankees (American)

CC. 'The' is used as a part of the title :

The mayor of a town

The duke of Westminster

The President of India

The King of Spain

DD. 'The' is not used before the abstract noun in general:

Life is beautiful.

Love is charming.

But it is used before the abstract noun that refers to a definite person or thing:

This book describes the life of Mahatma Gandhi.

The love of Hamlet and Celia is illusory.

EE. Used before present participles or the gerunds and adjectives when they are used as nouns:

The meeting was successful.

The singing bird is there.

The talking man is coming.

Did you get the missing child?

FF. It is used when referring to an outstanding person, or event in phrases or titles:

Man of the match

Player of the year

Student of the year

GG. When a noun comes after a preposition, 'the' is always used.

The players are in the field.

The paintings are at the exhibition.

HH. 'The' is used before the comparative adjectives or adverbs:

The more I talk to you, the more I know you.

The more you go away, the more you miss her.

II. 'The' is used in some time expressing phrase:

One can get admission in the college anytime during the year.

I got up three in the morning today.

The day after tomorrow is a Sunday.

But no article is used before time expressing phrase like at afternoon, at night, last day, all night, all day, every year etc.

CHAPTER TWO

Indefinite Articles: A and An

Merriam Webster dictionary defines the article as any of a small set of words or affixes (as a, an, and the) used with nouns to limit or give definiteness to the application. It limits a noun or specifies it. An article, in the context of grammar, is a determiner. They don't exist independently of nouns. They do come with the nouns. Indefiniteness in English is expressed through a or an.

1. Indefinite articles are used before indefinite nouns.

There is a boy playing in the garden.

Could you give me a novel to read?

2. The article 'A' is used before singular, countable nouns which begin with consonant sounds.

He is a student.

He has a black pen.

Ramesh has a car.

We saw a tiger at the spot.

3. A or an is used before the countable noun when the hearer or reader does not know which one is referred to:

He was talking about a 9 years old boy.

There is a house on the street.

4. The article ‘an’ is used before singular, countable nouns which begin with vowel sounds.

Rashmi is an actress.

She had an umbrella.

She gave me an orange.

5. A or an refers to a singular countable noun. They are not used with plural nouns.

She had an umbrellas. (wrong).

She had an umbrella.(right)

6. A or an or the is used before the adjective that modifies a noun:

A beautiful umbrella

A female artist

The school boy

7. A or an should agree with the first sound of the adjective modifying a noun:

A beautiful umbrella (correct)

An beautiful umbrella (wrong)

8. ‘A’ is used before the words which start with consonant sound, although the first letter is a vowel.

a European university, a university

A is also used before the letters and numbers which sound like consonant but start with a vowel:

a euro, a one rupee note

9. An is used before such word that starts with a consonant letter but sounds like a vowel:

an hour, an honest man

10. In the case of acronyms, ‘an’ is used before the words whose first letter is pronounced as vowel, although the first letter is a consonant:

an MLA , an MP

11. There are differences in the use of a or an as far as the variety of English is concerned. In some British English,

'h' sound in hospital is silent, so some people use 'an' before hospital: an hospital

But very often in most of the varieties, 'a' is used before hospital.

12. A or an is not used before uncountable nouns in English: examples:

advice, salt, sugar, information

An advice (wrong), an information (wrong)

But when such uncountable nouns are specified with some determiner, a or an is used:

A piece of advice,

A piece of information

13. A and an are indefinite articles. This is why they are used before unspecified indefinite things:

I want a pen (a pen means any pen, not a specified one).

He reads a book. (a book means any book, the book is not a known book).

14. When something is introduced for the first time, a or an is used.

I am a teacher.(this is being introduced to the listener for the first time).

15. Generally, ' a', 'an' and 'the' are not used before the names of the diseases:

The medicine can be used to treat malaria.

He is doing research on cancer.

But 'the' is used before the names of some diseases like:

The measles, the flu, the mumps,

The bubonic plague

Some illnesses require a or an: A cold, a heart attack, a stroke, a tumor, a soar throat, a headache, a toothache

16. Articles are not used before the direction which follows a verb:

We need to go east.

Take left and get the house.

But when such direction follows a preposition, 'the' is used:

The school is in the south.

The shop is on the right.

CHAPTER THREE

No Article

A. No article is used before an uncountable noun (cannot be counted with numbers). They may be the names for abstract ideas, qualities or too small objects. As for examples: water, information, oil, sugar, rice, beauty, anger, money etc.

B. No article is used before the names of the people, books, art work, and places (village, town, city, country):

A Ram is standing there. (wrong)

The New York is a city. (wrong).

The students have read a Hamlet. (wrong)

If the name of a country contains words like States, Kingdom, Republic, Emirates, Union, Coast, the definite article, 'the' is used (refer to chapter 1).

C. No article is used before the names of the sports or games

They are playing cricket.

Tennis is a racket sport.

D. No article is used before breakfast, lunch, supper, dinner.

E. When a direction follows a verb, no article is used with the direction:

We travelled north all day.

He ran towards east and turned left.

The definite article is used before the direction that follows a preposition.

My school is on the south.

Have you ever stayed in the north?

Exercise-1

1. Find out the definite and indefinite article from the following extracts:

Friends, Romans, countrymen, lend me your ears;
I come to bury Caesar, not to praise him.
The evil that men do lives after them;
The good is oft interred with their bones;
So let it be with Caesar. The noble Brutus
Hath told you Caesar was ambitious:
If it were so, it was a grievous fault,
And grievously hath Caesar answer'd it.
Here, under leave of Brutus and the rest--
For Brutus is an honourable man;
So are they all, all honourable men--
Come I to speak in Caesar's funeral.- **Antony's speech, Julius Ceaser, William Shakespeare**

Alice was beginning to get very tired of sitting by her sister on the bank, and of having nothing to do: once or twice she had peeped into the book her sister was reading, but it had no pictures or conversations in it, `and what is the use of a book,' thought Alice `without pictures or conversation?'

So she was considering in her own mind (as well as she could, for the hot day made her feel very sleepy and stupid), whether the pleasure of making a daisy-chain would be worth the trouble of getting up and picking the daisies, when suddenly a White Rabbit with pink eyes ran close by her.

There was nothing so very remarkable in that; nor did Alice think it so very much out of the way to hear the Rabbit say to itself, `Oh dear! Oh dear! I shall be late!' (when she thought it over afterwards, it occurred to her that she ought to have wondered at this, but at the time it all seemed quite natural); but when the Rabbit actually took a watch out of its waistcoat-pocket, and looked at it, and then hurried on, Alice started to her feet, for it flashed across her mind that she had never before seen a rabbit with either a waistcoat-pocket, or a watch to take out of it, and burning with curiosity, she ran across the field after it, and fortunately was just in time to see it pop down a large rabbit-hole under the hedge. - **Alice's Adventures in Wonderland, Lewis Carroll**

2. Fill in the blanks with an appropriate article:

i) Matthew is reading _____ holy Bible.

ii) India is _____ multilingual country.

iii) He died of _____ heart-attack.

iv) Ramesh has___ umbrella.

v) My class teacher was reading ___book. _____ book was in the shelf.

vi) Mr. Das is _____ MLA.

vii) ___ Bay of Bengal is ___ largest bay in the world.

viii) My house is on___ south.

Ix) Could you please give me___ pen?

x) May I take ___ red pen?

xi) ___ more you read, __ more you learn.

Xii) In ___last cricket match, Tendulkar got man of__ match.

xiii) Mr.Russel is ___ university student.

xiv) I knew that he was __ mayor of a town.

xv) In ___ eighties, the poet was very active.

xvi) Sweta is __ sixth daughter of Mr.Das.

3. Supply the articles wherever required:

While we were in this condition - men yet laboring at oar to bring boat near shore - we could see(when, our boat mounting the waves, we were able to see the shore) great many people running along the strand to assist us when we should come near; but we made but slow way towards the shore; nor were we able to reach the shore till, being past the lighthouse at Winterton, shore falls off to westward towards Cromer, and so the land broke off a little the violence of the wind. Here we got in, and though not without much difficulty, got all safe on shore, and walked afterwards on foot to Yarmouth, where, as unfortunate men, we were used with great humanity, as well by magistrates of the town, who assigned us good quarters, as by particular merchants and owners of ships, and had money given us sufficient to carry us either to London or back to Hull as we thought fit. **-pg no 15, Robinson Crusoe, Daniel Defoe**

4. Strike out the wrong one from the underlined phrases:

A. A Konark is in Odisha.

B. It is the big building in the city.

C. He gave me an advice.

D. I have a one rupee note.

E. The USA is a big country.

F. Will you have the lunch, please?

5. Fill in the blanks:

My grandfather was sitting in ___chair. He was reading__magazine. ___ magazine was about ___working women in a city. While reading____magazine, he asked for __ cup of tea. My grandfather was at__age of eighty. Whenever I got time, I gossiped with him. He was narrating me about___ story of __ woman freedom fighter. She was staying in ___ rural village. She was encouraging ___ villagers to fight for their rights.

CHAPTER FOUR

Demonstratives

The Oxford dictionary of English defines demonstrative as indicating a person or a thing referred to. In English, there are four demonstratives: this, these, that, and those. Look at the following examples:

This is a book. This is a school.

That is a boy. That is a house.

These are tables. These are temples.

Those are balls. Those are pipes.

A. This

i) This is used to refer to something or someone that is near you:

This is the man who inspired me.

This is the file I am looking for.

ii) While introducing people, we use 'this'.

This is Rinky and this is Renu.

iii) 'This' is used to refer to an idea or situation mentioned in the previous context or sentences or conversation:

You would have avoided this situation, had you gone there.

iv) It is used to refer to the place where someone is at present:

I don't belong to this country.

v) 'This' is used to refer to the present day or present month or festival that is forthcoming:

They will visit home this summer.

vi) 'This' is used when someone indicates the size or shape of something with his/her hands:

I just looked back and found this big dog next to us.

B. These

i)This is used for singular noun. Its plural form is 'these'. 'These' is used before the plural nouns:

These boys were playing in the garden.

ii) It is used before nouns about which one is going to talk:

Do you have these books with you?

iii) One uses 'these' to refer to people or things near to him/her:

These are horror movies.

C. That

i) That is used to refer to something or someone that is away in position or in time:

That boy whom we met that day was a college student.

It is used to refer to the more distant of two things near to the speaker.

This child is smarter than that child.

ii) It is used to refer to the things or ideas mentioned before:

How was that idea?

iii) That is used for identifying someone or something.

That is my daughter in a red dress.

iv) That is used to refer back to something someone said or did:

Shall we go for lunch? Yes, that is a good idea.

D. Those

'Those' is the plural form of that. Look at the following examples:

That is a dog. Those are dogs.

That is a house. Those are houses.

i) 'Those' is used to refer to the plural noun.

Those are my note books.

I am referring to those boys who were attending my last class.

ii) It is used to refer to the things or people which are away from the speaker in time and space:

Could you please explain about those books in the shelf?

Exercise-2

A. Fill in the blanks with appropriate word from the bracket:

i) Could you please pass me ___sticks? (this /these)

ii) What was __idea you shared with me yesterday? (this /that)

iii) You should read___book on the table. (this /that)

iv) ____flowers smell good. (these /this)

B. Find out the demonstrative determiners from the following passages:

Passage:1

It is a truth universally acknowledged that a single man in possession of a good fortune, must be in want of a wife.

However little known the feelings or views of such a man may be on his first entering a neighborhood, this truth is so well fixed in the minds of the surrounding families, that he is considered the rightful property of someone or other of their daughters. ***(From chapter-1, Pride and Prejudice, Jane Austen)***

Passage:2

"And you hens, how many eggs have you laid in this last year, and how many of those eggs ever hatched into chickens? The rest have all gone to market to bring in money for Jones and his men. And you, Clover, where are those four foals you bore, who should have been the support and pleasure of your old age? Each was sold at a year old — you will never see one of them again. In return for your four confinements and all your labour in the fields, what have you ever had except your bare rations and a stall?"***(From chapter-1, Animal Farm, George Orwell)***

CHAPTER FIVE

Possessive Determiners

A possessive determiner is a word that shows what someone or something has or with what someone or something is related. All the personal pronouns are having possessive determiners like *my, your, his, her, its, our, your, their*. These determiners modify a noun and are used before a noun.

<u>My</u> house is there.

Is this <u>your</u> coat?

Graham wrote in <u>his</u> note book.

A. My

'My' is used to refer to a speaker's possession:

Rahim came to my house.

Shekhar is looking at my bike.

B. Your

'Your' is used to refer to the belongingness of the person to whom someone is addressing:

Can I take your umbrella?

'Your father is coming here.'

C. His

'His' is used to indicate that something belongs to a male person:

The boy is in this school. His father is a teacher and his mother is a doctor.

D. Her

'Her' is used to indicate that something belongs to a female person:

Could you please show me her dress?

E. Its

'Its' is used to indicate that something belongs to a thing, place, animal, child or a baby:

The institution celebrates its annual day.

F. Our

'Our' is used to show that something belongs to the people in general including the speaker himself/herself:

The success of our work depends on you.

G. Your

'Your' is used to refer to something that belongs to someone whom the speaker is addressing or talking to:

Who is your father?

Could you show me your hand?

H. Their

It is used to refer to something that belongs to or related to a group of people, animal or things:

The students will write their exams.

Exercise-3

1. Find out the possessive determiners from the following passages:

My father's family name being Pirrip, and my Christian name Philip, my infant tongue could make of both names nothing longer or more explicit than Pip. So, I called myself Pip, and came to be called Pip.

I give Pirrip as my father's family name, on the authority of his tombstone and my sister - Mrs. Joe Gargery, who married the blacksmith. As I never saw my father or my mother, and never saw any likeness of either of them (for their days were long before the days of photographs), my first fancies regarding what they were like, were unreasonably derived from their tombstones. The shape of the letters on my father's, gave me an odd idea that he was a square, stout, dark man, with curly black hair. From the character and turn of the inscription, 'Also Georgiana Wife of the Above,' I drew a childish conclusion that my mother was freckled and sickly. To five little stone lozenges, each about a foot and a half long, which were arranged in a neat row beside their grave, and were sacred to the memory of five little brothers of mine - who gave up trying to get a living, exceedingly early in that universal struggle - I am indebted for a belief I religiously entertained that they had all been born on their 2 of 865 Great Expectations backs with their hands in their trousers-pockets, and had never taken them out in this state of existence. (chapetr-1, **Great Expectations, Charles Dickens**)

2. Supply the appropriate determiner in the blanks:

i) The girl is showing ___ dress to __ friends.

ii) I was talking to Rakesh. __ father was a doctor.

iii) The students showed me___school.

iv) We are ready to distribute___ books to the students.

CHAPTER SIX

Quantifiers

A quantifier is a word or phrase to indicate the amount or quantity of a noun. The following is a list of quantifiers in English: *some, any, few, little, more, much, many, each, every, both, all, enough, half, whole, less.*

A) Some

i) It is used to indicate the quantity that is not precise or specified:

Some boys are absent today.

Can you get me some books?

ii) With plural and uncountable nouns:

I have some ideas to share.

Could you please give me some information?

The teacher gives me some time to discuss about the question.

iii) Refers to a small number of people or a part of something:

Some people in the village are suffering from malaria.

Some portions of the film will be shot in New York.

iv) Used to indicate an approximate number:

Some 20 years ago I visited your city.

The garden is some 5 kilometers away.

v) Used with affirmative sentences:

There are some doctors in the hospital who treat well.

Some teachers were using this method.

vi) Used in offering something or asking for something:

Would you like some tea?, Can I have some biscuit, please?

B) Any

i) Used in negative sentences with plural and uncountable nouns:

He does not have any information.

ii) Used in questions:

Do you have any friends here?

Is there any shop in the village?

C) Few

i) 'A few' is used to refer to a small number of people or things:

He has a few friends here.

He got votes from a few people.

ii) 'Few' refers to not many or almost none:

She had few minutes to see her mother.

iii) 'Few' is used with plural countable nouns:

Few students came to school.

D) Little

i) Little is used to refer to 'not much' or almost nothing:

He gave me little water.

ii) Little is used with uncountable nouns:

There was little sugar.

iii) 'A little' is used with singular uncountable nouns:

He ate a little bread.

E) More

It is the comparative form of much and many.

i) Used to indicate that there is a greater amount of something than before:

He will spend more time on the task.

More people will join the party soon.

You have more rice to eat.

ii) More is used with the adjectives of more than one syllable:

His book is more enlightening than the book I gave you yesterday.

F) Much

It is used to indicate a large amount of something. It is used with singular uncountable nouns.

There is much water in the well.

ii) Much is used with negative and question sentences:

He doesn't have much money.

There was not much crop in the field.

iii) Much is used to indicate the degree of something:

How much protein do you take every day?

G) Many

i) It is used to refer to a large number of people or thing. It is used with plural nouns.

Many people will vote for him.

Many villages in the area don't have electricity.

ii) Used with question sentences :

How many students are there?

H) Each

i) It refers to any individual in a group or a thing in the aggregate:

Each student has a pen.

Each of the books has many pictures.

I) Every

i) It is used to refer to all the members of a group or all the parts of something.

Every city has a bus-stop.

ii) Every shows the regular interval of space and time:

Every five minutes he calls me.

Every ten kilometers you will get a shop.

We meet in the garden every Sunday evening.

iii) Every one of is used before a pronoun in objective form or a determiner.

Every one of the staff wants to go out.

iv) 'Every' is used before a number:

Five out of every ten students scored well.

One out of every four doctors is skilled.

J) Both

i) 'Both' refers to two people or things together:

Both teachers are good at Mathematics.

Both books were on the table.

ii) Both or both of can be used before a determiner:

He took both my books/ He took both of my books.

They are both her brothers/ They are both of her brothers.

iii) 'Both' is used in between a subject and a main verb:

We both want to speak to the manager.

You both take time and do the work.

iv) It is used after be verb as a main verb in a sentence:

They were both very nice and gentle.

v) Used after the first auxiliary or modal verb:

We might both have been forgotten.

K) All

i) All refers to everything of a group or everyone of a group.

All people will be present there.

All shops are opened today.

ii) Used to refer to the whole amount or quantity:

He gave away all his property.

The leader could not sleep all night.

iii) Used to refer to more than one person or thing:

Who all did you invite to the party?

iv) Used to refer to the whole of a period of time:

They will write exam all afternoon.

I was sick all morning.

The teacher is teaching all week.

L) Enough

i) It is used to refer to as much as one needs.

Raju had enough money to travel.

I have enough work.

ii) While modifying an adjective or adverb, it comes after the adjective or adverb.

Are you cold enough?

He is young enough to do the task.

iii) When it modifies an adjective and a noun together, enough is used before the adjective:

The boy had collected enough big bottles.

M) Half

i) Half is used to refer to the whole group divided in two. It can be used with nouns preceded by a, an, and the.

Half the students are already absent.

Half of a watermelon is enough for you.

ii) It is also used with possessive pronouns.

Half of my notebook is wet.

Half of our people are not educated.

iii) Refers to a measurement or time and used with indefinite articles:

He walks half a kilometer every day.

You bought half a kilo of sugar.

N) Whole

i) It is used before nouns when talk about quantity in completeness and used after other determiners:

The symptom is found in the whole of eastern India.

My whole life is spent on reading the Bhagavad Gita.

The whole month of April was about the flowers in the city.

O) Less

i) Used to show that there is a smaller amount of something than before and used as the comparative form of little.

He is less active than before.

ii) It is used with uncountable nouns.

You have given less water to the trees.

I have less money.

He has spent less time in reading the novel.

Exercise-4

1. Fill in the blanks:

i) _____10 years ago I saw him in the town.

ii) They don't have ___ book.

iii) Could you please give me _____ information?

iv) The tea is sweet. _____ sugar is added to it.

v) Is there___ hospital in the village?

vi) The movie is ___ interesting than the one we watched last Sunday.

vii) The flower trees are dying. You are giving___ water to the trees.

viii) He was not poor ___ to be selected for the grant.

ix) How___ students are there?

2. Complete the paragraph:

My father was searching two books on banking that he purchased last week. ___ books would be of help for him. ___ of the books is full of graphs and equations. These books are good out of ___ten books on banking. ___ of his colleagues have read these books.

CHAPTER SEVEN

Other Determiners

Either

It refers to any one of the two mentioned in a sentence. It is used before a singular noun.

Would you like to come on Saturday or Sunday? I would come on either day.

I am not interested in either book.

Neither

Neither refers to each of the two people or things mentioned when something about them is not true or negative and it is used before singular countable noun:

Neither boy could compete.

Neither man speaks English.

Numerals

Numerals are determiners that are used before a noun. There are two kinds of numerals: A) Cardinal- expresses quantity like one, ten, hundred, 1, 10 etc, B) Ordinal- expresses sequence like first, second, third etc.

i) Cardinal numbers:

Ten people were present there.

They have selected 200 colleges for using the methodology.

ii) Ordinal numbers:

He came first in the examination.

They will give him the third prize.

The words like next, last are also ordinal numbers which express sequence:

My father is coming back next week.

I got my Bachelor degree last year.

Exercise-5

1. Complete the sentences with suitable determiners:

i) He passed the teacher-ship examination ___ year.

ii) We will be going abroad___ week.

iii) There was no support on___ side.

iv) George Washington was the ___ president of the United States.

2. Correct the following sentences:

i) Neither student write good English.

ii) Thomas does not like either books.

iii) Either you or me can speak to him.

References

Austen, Jane. 1813/1894. *Pride and Prejudice*. London: Whitehall & George Allen.

Carroll, Lewis. 1865. *Alice's Adventures in Wonderland*. London: Macmillan.

Elster, Charles Harrington. 1999. *The Big Book of Beastly Mispronunciations*. Boston: Houghton Mifflin Harcourt.

Crystal, David.2003. *The Cambridge Encyclopedia of the English Language*. Cambridge: Cambridge University Press.

Dickens, Charles. 1860/1996. Great Expectations. London:Penguin Books.

Definite Article: the. 1999-2014.englisch-hilfen.de. Accessed on 4 August,2014: www.englisch-hilfen.de

Defoe, Daniel. 1981. *Robinson Crusoe*. First published in 1719. New York: Bantam Classics.

Kolln, Martha & Robert Funk. 1998. *Understanding English Grammar*. Boston: Allyn and Bacon.

Nordquist, Richard. 2019. *Definition and Uses of the Definite Article 'the' in English*. Accessed online: https://www.thoughtco.com/definite-article-grammar-1690423

Mc Arthur, Tom.(Ed.). 1998. *Oxford Concise Companion to the English Language*. Oxford: Oxford University Press.

Matthews, P.H. 2007. *Oxford Concise Dictionary of Linguistics*. Oxford: Oxford University Press.

Orwell, George. 1946. *Animal Farm*. New York: Harcourt, Brace and company.

Shakespeare, William. 1902. The Tragedy of Julius Caesar. First published in 1599. London: Methuen.

The Definite Article: the. 2014. British Council. Accessed on 27 July, 2014: learnenglish.britishcouncil.org

The OEC: Facts about the Language. Oxford University Press. Accessed on 19 July 2014: <http://www.oxforddictionaries.com/words/the-oec-facts-about-the-language>.

Word Frequency Data, Corpus of Contemporary American English. Accessed online: www.wordfrequency.info.

World English, 1999-2003. The One Stop Resource for the English Language. World English. Accessed on 17 July, 2014: www.world-english.org.

9 798885 464406

Printed by Libri Plureos GmbH in Hamburg,
Germany